Pre-Level I

Rebecca W. Keller, Ph.D.

Text illustrations: Janet Moneymaker
Marjie Bassler

Astronomy Pre-Level I Textbook-Softcover

ISBN # 978-1-936114-11-5

Published by Gravitas Publications, Inc.
4116 Jackie Road SE, Suite 101
Rio Rancho, NM 87124

www.gravitaspublications.com

Chapter 1: Exploring the Cosmos

WOO HOO!

1.1 Introduction

When you look up at the sky at night, what do you see? If the sky is free of clouds and there are not too many lights around, you might see the Moon, stars, planets, and if you are lucky, a comet!

Astronomy is the study of the cosmos. The term cosmos refers to Earth and everything that extends beyond Earth, including other planets, stars, nebulae, comets, asteroids, and even black holes.

Because astronomers can't fly to far away planets or ride asteroids to study them, astronomers use various tools and techniques to find out more about the objects in the cosmos. We will learn more about these tools in Chapter 2. However, even before the use of modern tools, people could learn a great deal about the cosmos by studying the night sky.

1.2 Who Was the First Astronomer?

It's hard to say who was the first astronomer. Many early people studied the planets and stars and even without modern tools discovered a great deal about the cosmos.

Early Egyptian, Babylonian, and Mayan people observed the sky in great detail. Noting when the Moon was full or when the Sun sank lower on the horizon, early observers were able to learn about how the planets and the Moon moved. From their observations they produced calendars and were even able to predict eclipses. We will learn more about eclipses in Chapter 3.

One of the questions early astronomers asked was, "Does the Earth move around the Sun, or does the Sun move around the

Earth?" In other words, do we live in a "Sun-centered" cosmos or an "Earth-centered" cosmos? It appears, from simple observation, that we live in an Earth-centered cosmos. When the Sun rises and sets each day, it has the appearance of moving around the Earth. However, as we will see, sometimes how things move isn't always easy to figure out.

One of the very first astronomers to propose that the Earth moves around the Sun was Aristarchus of Samos. Aristarchus was a Greek astronomer and mathematician who lived from 301-230 BCE. He studied the planets and said that the Earth has two different movements. One movement is that Earth travels around the Sun, and the other movement is that Earth revolves around its own axis. We now know that he was right! But during his time no one believed him. It would be almost 2000 years before astronomers would look closely at his ideas.

1.3 Famous Early Astronomers

Nicolaus Copernicus was a famous astronomer who also thought that the Earth moved around the Sun. Copernicus was born in 1473 in the ancient Polish city of Torun. During the time Copernicus lived, most scientists believed that the Sun revolved around the Earth. They believed that the Earth was the center of the universe and everything revolved around it.

Copernicus did not agree with the scientists of his day. His ideas would eventually change the whole science of astronomy! Unlike Aristarchus, Copernicus was able to use mathematics to show that the Earth moves around the Sun and that the Sun remains fixed in one location. However, Copernicus was not outspoken about his ideas. Because he knew his ideas might upset people, he didn't talk about them. When Copernicus did publish his work, a few people got upset, but most people just ignored his hard work. Another 100 years passed before people took his ideas seriously.

Another famous astronomer also changed the way we see the cosmos. His name was Tycho Brahe. Tycho was

born in 1546 in the Danish town of Scania, and he was raised by his uncle. Like Copernicus, Tycho was curious about astronomy. His uncle wanted him to be a lawyer or a politician, but Tycho studied mathematics and slipped away at night to look at the sky. When his uncle died, Tycho was free to pursue his interests in astronomy.

Telescopes were not yet invented (see Chapter 2), so Tycho used sighting tubes, which are just hollow tubes with no lenses. Tycho discovered that stars do not always stay the same but are constantly changing. Based on his observations, Tycho decided to rewrite the map of the stars and spent his life working on his ideas.

Galileo Galilei was also a famous early astronomer. He was interested in trying to find out how the planets move. Galileo was born in 1564 in Pisa, Italy. He studied many different subjects, such as mathematics and physics, and he loved to look at the stars. Galileo used his knowledge of math and physics to better understand how the planets and the Moon move.

Like Copernicus, Galileo was an independent thinker, and he didn't believe in an Earth-centered universe. Galileo did experiments because he wanted to show how things moved rather than just coming up with ideas about it. By doing experiments and by using mathematics and physics, Galileo was able to prove that we live in a Sun-centered solar system that is made up of the Sun and the objects traveling around it. Being able to prove an idea by using experiments, math, and physics was the beginning of astronomy as a science.

1.4 Astronomers Today

Today many scientists study the stars and planets. Astronomy is a science, and modern astronomers are scientists who use a variety of scientific tools and scientific techniques to learn about the

universe. In Chapter 2 we will learn more about the tools astronomers use.

However, even with new tools, modern astronomers must use the same basic skills that Copernicus, Tycho, and Galileo used.

Today's astronomers must make good observations and must train themselves to see the details, like Copernicus did. Astronomers must also study math and physics like Tycho and Galileo did. Math and physics are essential for understanding how the stars and planets move in space. Most importantly, astronomers must always be curious and willing to argue to defend their ideas like Copernicus, Tycho, and Galileo did.

1.5 Summary

● Astronomy is the study of space and all the objects found in space.

● Early astronomers were able to discover a great deal about the stars and planets by using observation.

● Nicolaus Copernicus, Tycho Brahe, and Galileo Galilei were three early astronomers who changed the way we understand the universe.

● Modern astronomers still use observation, math and physics to study space.

Chapter 2: The Telescope

2.1 Introduction

When Copernicus was gazing at the night sky, looking up at the stars and wondering about the cosmos, he had to do all of his investigating without the help of a telescope. Copernicus was smart, and he revolutionized the way we think about the universe. But without being able to see the details of planets, their moons, and the Sun, Copernicus was limited in what he could explore.

Galileo was exploring the skies, just like Copernicus, but Galileo was born during the time when the telescope was being invented. In the early 1600's Galileo found out about a spyglass that a Dutch lens grinder named Hans Lippershey had invented. Galileo knew that this spyglass could help him study the cosmos by helping him see things that were far away.

Galileo used the ideas that Lippershey had come up with and created his own spyglasses that would eventually become the telescope.

2.2 What Is a Telescope?

A telescope is a tool or instrument that helps astronomers see far into the distance. A simple telescope has two lenses connected by a long tube.

One lens is called the eyepiece and is located at one end of the tube. You look through this lens with your eye.

Eyepiece   Long Tube   Objective Lens

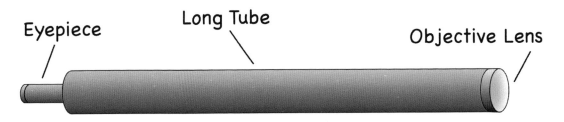

The other lens is called the objective lens and is located at the other end of the tube. The objective lens is used to collect light so an object may be viewed.

As light travels through the objective lens and down the tube, it is focused by the eyepiece. In this way the object being viewed becomes magnified, or made to appear larger. The larger the objective lens, the more light can be collected, and the longer the tube, the larger the object will appear.

2.3 Early Telescopes

Early telescopes looked very much like the simple telescope in the previous section. Early telescopes were often made of metal, such as brass or copper, with two simple lenses, one at either end of a long tube.

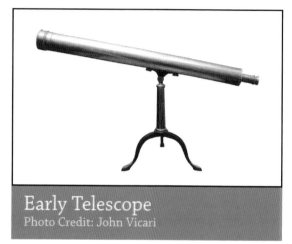

Early Telescope
Photo Credit: John Vicari

The body of the metal tube was sometimes attached to a stand. The astronomer could pivot the telescope on its stand, adjusting the direction in which the telescope was pointing.

Gregorian Telescope
Photo: © Dorotheum, May 2011, Lot 40

Another type of early telescope was called the Gregorian telescope or Newtonian telescope. This type of telescope not only had lenses, but also mirrors. Part of the problem with early telescopes was that in order to see a really far away object, the tube had to be very long. However, if the light was focused in a different way, far away objects could be seen with a shorter tube.

The Gregorian telescope used mirrors and lenses to focus the light. The light came in through the objective lens but then got bounced back and up into the eyepiece by the mirrors. This design helped astronomers use shorter telescopes to see distant objects.

2.4 Modern Telescopes

The telescope has come a long way from the spyglass of Galileo's day. Technological advances have resulted in significant improvements for the modern telescope. Today, astronomers can see not only the planets and their moons in our own solar system, but also planets and moons in other solar systems!

A galaxy is a large group of solar systems, stars, and other objects in space. Using modern telescopes, astronomers can now see whole solar systems, not only in Earth's galaxy, but in other galaxies as well!

One of the most famous modern telescopes is the Hubble Space Telescope. As the name suggests, the Hubble Space telescope is actually in space orbiting the Earth. The Hubble Space Telescope was launched into space in 1990 and has produced some of the most amazing images of space we have ever seen. In coming chapters we will see some of the amazing images that have been taken with the Hubble Space Telescope.

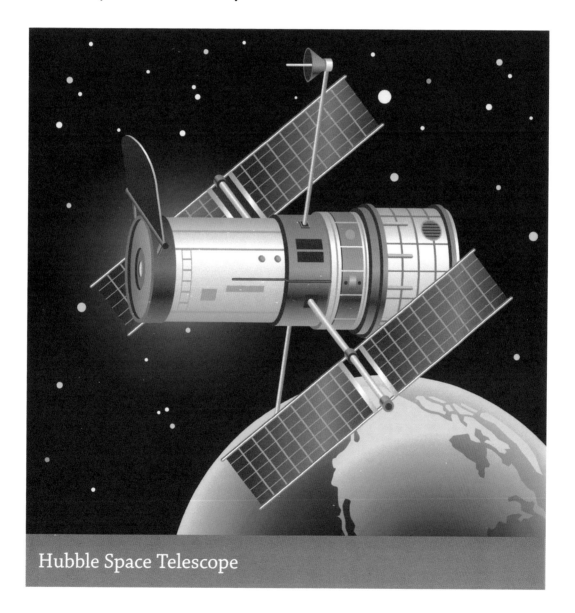

Hubble Space Telescope

2.5 Summary

- Astronomers use an instrument called a telescope to see far away objects.

- Galileo modified a spyglass to create the first telescope.

- Early telescopes had an objective lens and an eyepiece that were connected by a long tube.

- The Hubble Space Telescope is a modern telescope that is in space and travels around the Earth.

Chapter 3: Earth's Home in Space

COWABUNGA!

3.1 Introduction

Now that we know what astronomy is and how to study planets and stars, it's time to explore what Earth looks like from space.

Because Earth is so big compared to our human size, it's hard to imagine what Earth looks like from space. Is Earth the biggest object in space? Is Earth in the center of space? If we took a rocket into space, what would we find?

3.2 Earth Is a Planet

If you launched a rocket and traveled past the clouds into space, you would see the Earth. Earth would look like a blue marble floating in the dark space around it.

Earth is a planet. A planet has special properties. A planet has to be large enough to have its own gravity, which is the force that holds everything to the Earth's surface. A planet also has to move in space around a sun. And finally, a planet is shaped like a ball. Spherical is the word for ball-shaped.

Because Earth is very large, moves around the Sun in space, has gravity, and is spherical, Earth is called a planet.

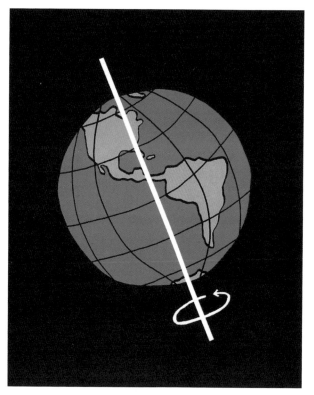

Earth rotates around an axis, which is an imaginary line that goes through the center of an object. If you took a ball and spun it with your fingers, it would rotate around an axis.

The Sun shines on different parts of Earth as Earth rotates. This is how we get our days and nights.

It takes 24 hours for Earth to rotate once around its axis. We don't feel the rotation of the Earth because the Earth's gravity holds down the air and everything else that's on Earth. Everything is moving at the same speed, and the Earth's rotation does not cause wind.

The Earth is tilted on its axis. "Tilted" means the Earth is not just straight up and down but is slanted. The tilt of Earth's axis gives us seasons.

For part of the year, the northern part of Earth is tilted towards the Sun and the southern part of the Earth is tilted away from the Sun. This gives the northern part of the Earth summer and the southern part winter.

Then, during a different part of the year, the southern part of the Earth is tilted towards the Sun and the northern part away from the Sun. When this happens, the southern part of Earth has summer, and the northern part has winter.

3.3 The Moon and Tides

If you take your rocket into space, you might run into the Moon. A moon is an object that travels around a planet. Our Moon is smaller than Earth and travels around Earth.

Our Moon does have some gravity and is spherical, but because it moves around Earth and not around the Sun as the Earth does, the Moon is not a planet. We will learn more about the Moon in Chapter 4.

Did you know that the Moon helps create ocean tides on Earth? It's true! The Moon pulls on Earth with some gravity. This pulling on the Earth causes the water in the oceans to be pulled too. As the Moon moves around the Earth, it pulls the ocean water

with it. The pulling of ocean water by the Moon helps create tides.

3.4 The Sun and Weather

If you wear sandals during a summer day, you can feel the Sun warming your toes. The Sun is a big ball of fire that gives light and heat energy to Earth.

The Earth orbits the Sun. The word orbit means to "revolve around." An orbit is the path one object makes as it travels around another object. If you stand with your hand on a pole and then start walking, you will make a path around the pole. You will orbit the pole. This is what Earth does as it moves around the Sun. We will learn more about the Sun in Chapter 4.

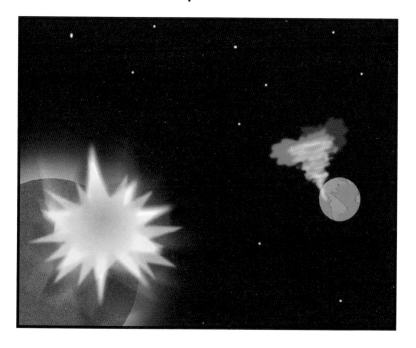

Did you know there are storms on the Sun? Did you know that the storms on the Sun can cause storms on Earth? It's true! Sun storms can contribute to Earth storms. Scientists who research weather can study Sun storms to find out how they affect Earth's weather.

3.5 Eclipses

During the Moon's orbit around Earth, the Moon travels behind the Earth. Then the Earth is in between the Moon and the Sun, and the Earth can block the Sun's light from reaching the Moon. When the Earth's shadow is cast on the Moon, it is called a lunar eclipse.

At other times, the Moon will be in between the Sun and the Earth. With the Moon in this position, the Moon can block the Sun's light from reaching a portion of the Earth. This is called a solar eclipse.

3.6 Summary

● Earth is a planet.

● One rotation of the Earth on its axis takes 24 hours (one day).

● Earth is tilted on its axis giving us seasons.

● The Moon and Sun affect Earth's tides and weather.

Chapter 4: Earth's Neighbors Moon and Sun

4.1 Introduction

We saw in Chapter 3 that the Earth sits in space. We also saw that the Moon and Sun cause changes in our ocean tides and weather. But what is a moon or a sun?

4.2 The Moon

You can see the Moon from Earth. If you look outside your house, you might see a bright, round shape in the sky. This is the Moon.

You can sometimes see the Moon during the day, but most often you see the Moon as the brightest object in the sky at night.

The Moon is spherical like the Earth but much smaller. The Moon has a very different surface from that of Earth. Although the Moon is made of rocks and minerals like Earth, the Moon cannot support life. It has very little oxygen and no liquid water.

The Moon looks bright in the sky, but the Moon does not generate its own light. Acting like a mirror, the Moon reflects the Sun's light to Earth.

The Moon orbits the Earth once a month. If you look at the Moon often, you will see that it appears to change its shape during the month. The different shapes are caused by different views of the Moon as we see it from Earth. The Moon can be round, half-round, or crescent shaped. When the Moon looks round, we say it is a full moon.

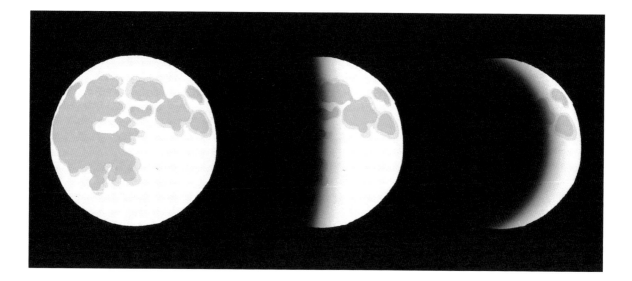

If you look closely at the Moon, you can see light and dark patches. These light and dark patches sometimes look like faces. The "Man in the Moon" is a famous nursery rhyme from Mother Goose.

The light and dark patches on the Moon are actually craters and lava flows.

4.3 The Sun

The other large object you see in the sky is the Sun. You can't look directly at the Sun (that would damage your eyes), but you can see that the Sun is rising in the morning, moving across the sky during the day, and setting at night.

The Sun is not a planet or a moon. The Sun is a star. A star is any object in space that generates its own light and heat energy (see Section 4.4).

The Sun is much larger than Earth. The Sun is so large that a million Earths would fit inside!

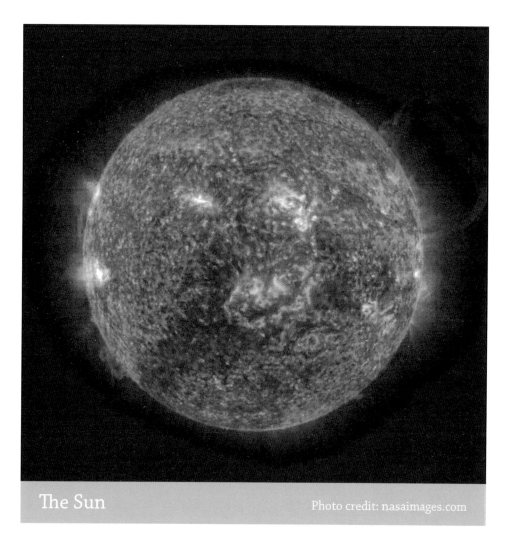

The Sun

Photo credit: nasaimages.com

The Sun is very hot. The temperature on the Sun's surface is thousands of times hotter than temperatures on Earth. The Sun is so hot that it would melt everything on Earth if Earth were too close to it!

4.4 The Sun's Energy

Our Sun generates its own light and heat energy. Because of this, the Sun is called a star. Recall that the Moon does not generate its own light.

The Sun is not made of rocks like the Earth and the Moon. Instead, the Sun is made of helium and hydrogen gases. The temperatures on the Sun are so hot that hydrogen atoms can stick together making helium atoms. When this happens, lots of light and heat energy is released.

We use the Sun's light and heat energy for food and fuel. Plants use the Sun's energy to make food, and we can use the Sun's energy to make electricity. Without the Sun there would be no life on Earth.

4.5 Summary

- The Moon orbits the Earth once a month.

- The Moon is made of rocks and minerals like Earth.

- Our Sun is a star and makes its own energy.

Chapter 5: Earth's Neighbors Planets

5.1 Introduction

In Chapter 4 we learned about two of Earth's neighbors—the Moon and the Sun. In this chapter we will learn about some of Earth's other neighbors—the planets.

5.2 Planets

If you look into the sky during the day, you can only see the bright Sun and possibly a very faded Moon.

But at night, depending on where you live, the sky lights up with brilliant specks of light. Many of these specks are stars, like our Sun. But some of the bright lights that dot the night sky are planets.

In Chapter 2 we found out that Earth is a planet. Remember that a planet is a spherical object that orbits a sun and is large enough to have gravity. Because the Moon orbits Earth, it is not a planet. Earth is a planet because it is large enough to have gravity, is spherical in shape, and orbits the Sun.

Earth is one of eight planets that orbit the Sun. The names of these eight planets are: Mercury, Venus, Earth, Mars, Jupiter, Saturn, Uranus, and Neptune.

5.3 Two Types of Planets

All of the planets are different from each other. Mercury has a barren moon-like surface, Venus has toxic gas clouds, and Saturn has brilliant rings. Mars has a reddish color, and Uranus and Neptune look blue or blue-green.

Even though all the planets are different from each other, some of the planets have features that are similar. Because of these similarities, scientist are able to separate the planets into two groups. The names of these two groups are terrestrial planets and Jovian planets.

Venus has toxic gas clouds

Jupiter is large and made of gas

Saturn has rings

Mercury has a moon-like surface

The terrestrial planets are those planets that are most like Earth, and the word terrestrial means "Earth-like." The terrestrial planets are: Mercury, Venus, Earth, and Mars.

All of the terrestrial planets are made of rock and minerals, like Earth. Also, all of the terrestrial planets have volcanoes, mountains, and craters on their surfaces.

However, of all the terrestrial planets, only Earth has life on it. Only Earth has the water, the oxygen, and the proper atmosphere needed to support life.

The Jovian planets are those planets that are similar to Jupiter. Jupiter is a very large planet made mostly of hydrogen gas and helium gas. All of the Jovian planets are like Jupiter because they are all very large and made mostly of gas. The Jovian planets are Jupiter, Saturn, Uranus, and Neptune.

5.4 Where's Pluto?

Pluto was once called the 9th planet, but in August 2006 scientists at the International Astronomical Union (IAU) changed their minds. They decided Pluto does not have all the features needed for it to be

classified as a planet. Pluto is now called a dwarf planet or a plutoid.

However, not all scientists agree with the IAU's decision. Scientists argue about conclusions all the time, and arguing is part of science. Someday Pluto may again be considered a planet.

5.5 Summary

- The eight planets are Mercury, Venus, Earth, Mars, Jupiter, Saturn, Uranus, and Neptune.

- The planets are separated into two groups: terrestrial planets and Jovian planets.

- Terrestrial planets are "like Earth" and are Mercury, Venus, Earth, and Mars.

- Jovian planets are "like Jupiter" and are Jupiter, Saturn, Uranus, and Neptune.

Chapter 6: Earth's Neighborhood

6.1 Introduction

In Chapter 5 we looked at two different types of planets. We found out that some of our planetary neighbors are Earth-like, and some are Jupiter-like. In this chapter we will take a look at where our planetary neighbors "live" in our solar neighborhood.

6.2 Our Solar Neighborhood

Most people live in some kind of neighborhood. A neighborhood is an area of town with houses, apartments, a few businesses, and possibly a park.

If you take a walk down the block in your neighborhood, you can see where your neighbors live. Some of your neighbors live close to you. Maybe they live next door and share the same backyard. Other neighbors live farther

away, but they may all go to the local grocery store or walk their dog in the local park. We would say that all of the people who live in this particular area of town are part of a neighborhood.

In the same way, planets share a particular area in space. All of the planets we explored in Chapter 5 share the area we call our solar system. A solar system is made up of a single sun and the planets and other objects that travel around that sun.

There are eight planets in our solar system. All of the planets share the same sun. Some planets are closer to our Sun, and some are farther away, just like the neighbors in your neighborhood.

The closest planet to the Sun is Mercury. Because Mercury is so close to the Sun, its surface can be very hot. The temperature at noon on Mercury can get up to as much as 800 degrees Fahrenheit! But Mercury does not have enough air to hold onto the heat from the Sun. At night the temperature on Mercury can go down to temperatures of below zero degrees Fahrenheit. So Mercury does not have the right temperatures for plants and animals to be able to live.

The next closet planet to the Sun is Venus. Venus is about twice as far away from the Sun as Mercury. However, even though Venus is farther from the Sun

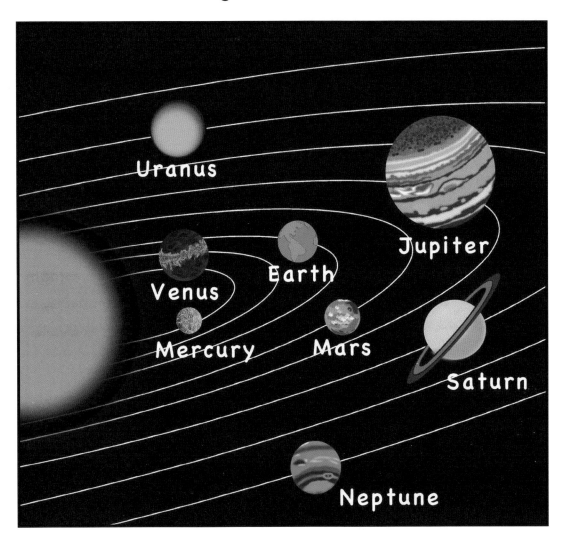

than Mercury, Venus is actually hotter! Venus has lots of carbon dioxide in the air which heats up the surface and holds the heat so Venus is hot all the time. The surface of Venus can reach over 860 degrees Fahrenheit. Venus is much too hot to support life.

The next closest planet to the Sun is Earth. Earth is close enough to the Sun to have enough heat for life to exist, but not so close that it is too hot for living things. Earth is the only planet in our solar system that supports life.

Mars sits farther away from the Sun than Earth does. Mars is much colder than Earth because it is farther away from the Sun. However, Mars is almost close enough to the Sun to support life.

Mercury, Venus, Earth, and Mars make up the inner solar system, or inner neighborhood. From an astronomer's perspective, all of these planets are relatively close to each other.

Much farther out are the four planets in the outer solar system. Jupiter is the first planet in the outer solar system. Jupiter is more than five times farther away from the Sun than Earth is.

Saturn is even farther away from the Sun than Jupiter is. Saturn is the second planet in the outer solar system. Uranus and Neptune are the last two planets in the outer solar system. Neptune is almost 30 times as far away from the Sun as Earth is. Jupiter, Saturn, Uranus, and Neptune are all much too cold to support life.

6.3 Orbits

The planets don't just sit in one spot, but move in a near circular orbit around the Sun. An orbit is a particular path, like a road, that a planet follows. Each planet stays in its orbit at its particular distance away from the Sun. Planets don't cross other planetary orbits or ever bump into each other.

Each planet takes a certain number of days to orbit the Sun. This is called a planetary year. Mercury orbits the Sun faster than does any other planet. It

Planet	Number of Days for One Orbit of the Sun
Mercury	88
Venus	225
Earth	365
Mars	687
Jupiter	4,332
Saturn	10,760
Uranus	30,700
Neptune	60,200

only takes 88 days for Mercury to complete one orbit. So one year on Mercury is only 88 days.

It takes Venus a little longer than Mercury to orbit the Sun, but not as long as it takes Earth. Venus orbits the Sun in 225 days, and Earth orbits the Sun in 365 days. The length of our calendar year is 365 days.

It takes Mars 687 days to orbit the Sun, and it takes Jupiter almost 12 Earth years to complete one planetary year!

Saturn takes almost 30 Earth years to orbit the Sun, and Uranus orbits the Sun in 84 Earth years. If you lived on Neptune you would need 165 Earth years just to get around the Sun once!

6.4 Why Is Earth Special?

Of all the planets in our solar system, only Earth is the right distance away from the Sun, with the right combination of water, oxygen, minerals, and soils to support life. Earth has just the right conditions for life to exist.

Earth has many unique features that make it just right for life. If Earth were closer to the Sun, it would be too hot for life. If Earth were farther away from the Sun, it would be too cold for life. If Earth's atmosphere had too much gas, like Venus does, it would cause the Earth's surface to heat up and would make it too hot.

Earth is special in this way. There is no other planet in our solar system that can support life. And so far no other planet in the universe has been found that supports life. Earth has just the right

temperature, is just the right distance from the Sun, and is made of just the right materials for life to exist!

6.5 Summary

- We live together with other planets in a planetary neighborhood called the solar system.

- All of the planets in our solar system share the same sun.

- Mercury is closest to the Sun, followed by Venus, Earth, Mars, Jupiter, Saturn, Uranus, and Neptune.

- Each planet rotates around the Sun in an orbit.

- Each planet takes a different number of days to complete one orbit around the Sun. The number of days it takes a planet to orbit the Sun once is called a planetary year. Our year is 365 days.

Chapter 7: Beyond the Neighborhood

7.1 Introduction

In Chapter 6 we looked at our planetary neighborhood called the solar system. We saw how the eight planets orbit the Sun and why Earth is the only planet in our solar system that can support life.

But what about other solar systems? What lies beyond our neighborhood? Are there other neighborhoods with suns like ours and planets like ours that support life?

7.2 Nearest Star

If you look up into the sky on a dark, clear night, you can see lots of stars. On a moonless night, far away from the city lights, you should be able to see at least 2000 stars.

The closest star to our Earth is a star called Proxima Centauri. Proxima Centauri is actually part of a three-star system. The two other stars in this system are called Alpha Centauri A and Alpha Centauri B. Alpha Centauri A, Alpha Centauri B, and Proxima Centauri orbit each other.

Proxima Centauri is smaller than our Sun and does not appear to have any planets orbiting it. Even though Proxima Centauri is the closest star to our Sun, it is not bright enough to be seen without a telescope. It does not appear to have any Earth-like planets or a solar system like ours.

7.3 Brightest Star

The brightest star is called Sirius. Sirius is farther away than Proxima Centauri but is brighter. The brightness of a star does not depend on how close it is, but on how much light the star makes.

One way to think about how much light a star makes is to look at the difference between a candle and a flashlight. A candle will light up or illuminate a few feet around it, but a flashlight can illuminate several yards. A flashlight puts out more energy than a candle and as a result can illuminate a much longer distance.

If you were to look at a candle and a flashlight from several yards away, the flashlight would look brighter. If you moved the flashlight a few yards farther away than the candle, it would still look brighter.

In the same way, Sirius is a brighter star than Proxima Centauri even though it is farther away.

7.4 Biggest Star

The biggest star is not necessarily the closest star or the brightest star. The biggest star we can see from Earth is called VY Canis Majoris or VY CMa.

VY CMa is about 2000 times larger than our Sun. If VY CMa were in our solar system, replacing our Sun, it would extend beyond the orbit of Saturn!

7.5 Stars With Planets

Hundreds of stars that have been studied seem to have planets orbiting them.

Astronomers can't see the planets directly. Planets are too dim and don't produce their own light like suns. However, astronomers can use other techniques to figure out if stars have planets orbiting them. One technique is to use physics to determine if a star is wobbling. As planets orbit a sun, their gravity pulls on the sun causing it to wobble. Astronomers can study a sun's wobble to determine if a planet might exist.

Hundreds of planets in other solar systems have been found, but so far none of them appear to be like Earth. In order for a planet to support life, it must be close to a sun but not too close. The sun must also be large enough to produce plenty of energy for the planet to use. But if the sun is too large, the planet will be too hot for living things to exist.

Scientists continue to search for life on other planets. So far, Earth is the only planet that we know supports life.

7.6 Summary

- Our nearest neighboring star is Proxima Centauri.

- The brightest star is Sirius.

- The largest star is VY Canis Majoris (VY CaM).

- So far, Earth is the only planet we know of that supports life.

Chapter 8: The Milky Way

8.1 Introduction

In Chapter 7 we looked at our nearby neighbors in the solar system. We saw that the closest star to our Sun is part of a three-star system and that the brightest star is not the star that is closest to us.

In this chapter we will take a look at nearby star systems that group together to form galaxies. Our Sun, our solar system, and neighboring stars are grouped together to make the Milky Way Galaxy.

8.2 A Solar City

On a clear night, far away from city lights, you can often see a band of stars across the night sky. All of these stars are in the Milky Way Galaxy.

The Milky Way is like a big city of stars, planets, dust and other objects. In a city, there are different neighborhoods, parks, shopping areas, and roads. All of these are grouped together to make a city. A city is organized in a certain way and has a certain shape that depends on how the neighborhoods, parks, shops and roads are put together.

The same is true of a galaxy. In a galaxy everything is held together by gravity. Like a big city, a galaxy holds all of the stars, planets, and other objects together in a particular shape. We will learn about the different shapes of galaxies in Chapter 9.

8.3 Our Galaxy

Can you see your whole city from your house? Is it easy to tell the shape of your city from where you live?

No. Because you are one small person in a big city, you can't tell what your city looks like from your house. You would need to see your city from a different place, like an airplane or spaceship, to tell what it looks like.

In the same way, it is difficult for astronomers to see the Milky Way Galaxy. No one has taken a picture of the Milky Way because it is too big and we can't fly far enough away to see it. However, astronomers can guess what the Milky Way Galaxy looks like by observing other galaxies.

Is our galaxy round or flat? Is our galaxy large or small? Does our galaxy have a fixed center, like an orange, or does it move like Jell-O?

Even though we've never seen our galaxy from outside of it, modern astronomers think that the Milky Way is shaped like a pinwheel. Just like a pinwheel, our galaxy has spiraling arms and a bulge in the center. This central bulge is a dense ball of stars. The arms of our galaxy are flatter at the edges than the center. Most of the stars in our galaxy are in the center, with fewer stars on the edges.

The Milky Way has two major arms, which are called the Scutum-Centaurus Arm and the Perseus Arm, and two minor arms, called the Norma Arm and the Sagittarius Arm. These arms spread out from the center, creating a spiral galaxy that looks like a pinwheel.

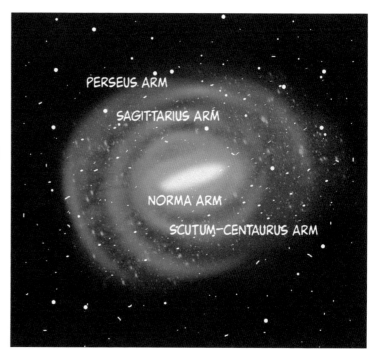

8.4 Where Are We?

Our Sun and solar system are located near the edge of our pinwheel-shaped galaxy, away from the center. We live on a partial arm called the Orion Arm. The Orion Arm is between the Sagittarius and Perseus arms.

We happen to live at just the right place in our galaxy. If our solar system were too far from the center of the galaxy, a planet like Earth might not be able to form. If our solar system were too close to the center, there might be too many stars creating too much radiation and gravity for life to form. As it turns out, we live in just the right place in our galaxy for life to exist—not too close to the center and not too far away!

8.5 Summary

- We live in the Milky Way Galaxy.

- A galaxy is a group of stars, solar systems, dust, and other objects held together by gravity.

- The Milky Way Galaxy looks like a pinwheel and is called a spiral galaxy.

- Our Earth is in just the right spot in our galaxy for life to exist.

Chapter 9: Beyond Our Galaxy

9.1 Introduction

In Chapter 8 we looked at our galaxy, the Milky Way. We saw that our galaxy is called a spiral galaxy and that it has a central bulge and has arms that extend outward from the center like a pinwheel.

In this chapter we will take a look at other types of galaxies. From Earth astronomers have been able to view thousands of different galaxies. Some of these  galaxies look like ours with a central bulge and spiral arms. But some galaxies look very different from our galaxy and have unusual features.

9.2 More Spiral Galaxies

There are many galaxies like ours. Spiral galaxies are fairly common in the universe. However, even spiral galaxies look different from one another.

The central bulge in some spiral galaxies is very spread out. This type of galaxy is called an Sa galaxy. Other spiral galaxies have a central bulge that is more compact. This type of galaxy is called an Sc galaxy.

Other spiral galaxies have a bar in their center. This type of spiral galaxy is called a barred spiral galaxy. Some astronomers think that the Milky Way Galaxy might be a barred spiral galaxy rather than a regular spiral galaxy.

9.3 Other Types of Galaxies

Astronomers have seen other types of galaxies that are different from spiral and barred spiral galaxies.

An elliptical galaxy is a type of galaxy that can look like one huge star but is really a group of tightly packed stars. Often, elliptical galaxies are smaller than spiral galaxies and have only a few thousand stars. However, there are a few elliptical galaxies that are very large and have billions of stars. Elliptical galaxies are round or elliptical in shape and don't have any special features.

Irregular galaxies don't look like spiral galaxies or elliptical galaxies. They don't really fit into any other category of galaxies and have a variety of odd features.

Some irregular galaxies have a large bulge of stars off to one side with a ring of stars surrounding it. Other irregular galaxies are dumbbell or butterfly shaped.

It's hard to know how some of these galaxies got their shape. Some astronomers think it might be possible that some of these irregular galaxies have such odd shapes because they are galaxies that have bumped into each other. But other astronomers think that the irregular shapes developed as the galaxies formed. Learning how galaxies form is an exciting area of modern astronomy.

9.4 The Local Group of Galaxies

Just as planets exist together around a star to form a solar system, and solar systems exist together to form galaxies, astronomers have discovered that galaxies exist together to form large groups. The Milky Way Galaxy is actually part of a large group of thirty

galaxies that are close together. Astronomers call this group of galaxies the Local Group.

The Milky Way is one of the three largest galaxies in the Local Group. Andromeda, our nearest neighboring galaxy, is the biggest of the three largest galaxies in the Local Group. And Triangulum is the smallest of the three largest galaxies in the Local Group.

9.5 Summary

- The three types of galaxies are spiral, elliptical, and irregular.

- Spiral galaxies can have large or small central bulges or a bar in the center.

- An elliptical galaxy can look like a big star but can contain thousands to billions of stars.

- Galaxies exist together to make large groups of galaxies.

Chapter 10:   Other Stuff in Space

LET'S GO CHECK OUT THE CRAB NEBULA

OKAY!

10.1 Introduction

In Chapter 9 we looked at different types of galaxies. We saw that some galaxies are like ours, with a central bulge and spiral arms. We also saw that some galaxies are irregular or elliptical.

What other things exist in the universe besides stars, planets, and galaxies?

10.2 Comets and Asteroids

Comets and asteroids are found throughout the universe.

Comets are large chunks of rock and ice that fly though space at great speeds. When a comet gets near a sun, the heat will make the ice in the comet begin to vaporize, creating a beautiful tail. When ice vaporizes, it changes to a gas without becoming liquid water first. You can notice the results of vaporization if you leave ice cubes in the freezer for a long time. They get smaller as the ice vaporizes.

Asteroids are made of rock and have irregular shapes. The Asteroid Belt is a ring of asteroids that travel around the Sun between the orbits of Mars and Jupiter. Many other asteroids exist outside the Asteroid Belt. Like comets, asteroids move through space at very high speeds. Most asteroids are small, and sometimes they collide with one another! As a result asteroids are often covered with small craters that are caused by these impacts.

Once in a while a comet or an asteroid will come close enough to Earth to hit it! If an asteroid hits Earth, it is called a meteorite. Although asteroids occasionally hit Earth, most of the time they burn up in our atmosphere before they reach the ground. If you have ever seen a shooting star, it is really an asteroid burning up as it flies through Earth's atmosphere.

10.3 Exploding Stars

Stars do not stay the same size or generate the same energy forever. Stars actually have a birth and a death. When a star is born, it is able to generate light and heat energy for a very long period of time. However, at some point it runs out of energy and dies. When this happens, the star gets very large, burning brighter and brighter. Astronomers call this type of star a red giant. Once the red giant star uses up all its energy, it shrinks into a small white dwarf star.

Sometimes stars actually explode. A supernova is a star that is exploding. When a supernova star explodes, it becomes very large and bright, expanding many millions of miles into the surrounding area.

10.4 Collapsed Stars

What happens to the exploding star once it has finished exploding? Where does it go? Does it turn into nothing, or does it become something else?

Many astronomers think that after a star explodes, a black hole might form. A black hole is an odd feature in the universe. It is difficult

to see a black hole because it doesn't allow any radio waves or light waves to bounce back from it. Because of this, it just looks like there is a dark, black hole in the middle of space.

10.5 Nebulae

By using the Hubble Space Telescope, astronomers can explore the universe in ways never before possible. The Hubble Telescope has given us some very beautiful pictures of stars, planets, asteroids, and galaxies.

Some of the most beautiful images captured by the Hubble Telescope are nebulae. Nebulae are clouds of gas, dust, and particles. The gas, dust, and particles swirl in space to create amazing celestial sculptures and cosmic art. Today several thousand nebulae have been photographed with the Hubble Telescope.

However, we have only just begun imaging, understanding, and discovering the stars, planets, and other objects that exist in space. Future generations of astronomers have a whole universe to discover and explore!

10.6 Summary

- Comets are objects in space that are made of rock and ice.

- Asteroids are objects in space that are made of rock and have irregular shapes. If an asteroid makes contact with Earth, it is called a meteorite.

- A star that explodes is called a supernova.

- Black holes are believed to be collapsed supernova stars.

- Nebulae are clouds of gas, dust, and particles.